TUDOR
1485–1603

STUART
1603–171

TORIAN
87–1901

MODERN TIMES
1901–NOW

children's HISTORY of
SUSSEX

Written by
Alison Milford

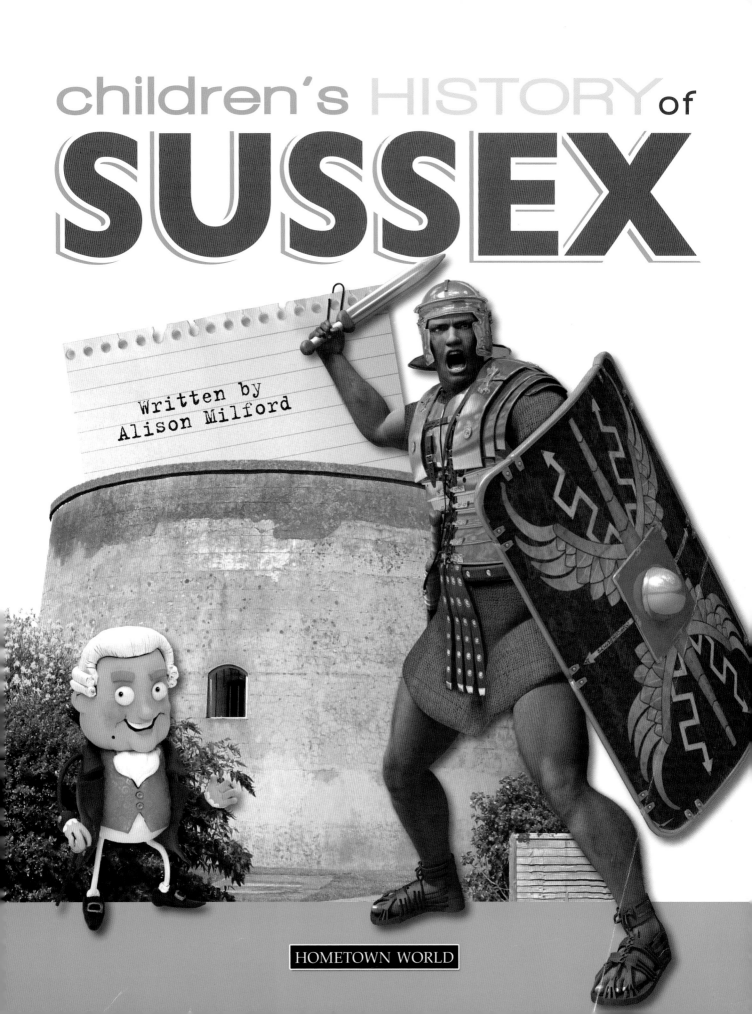

HOMETOWN WORLD

How well do you know Sussex?

Have you ever wondered what it would have been like living in Sussex when the Romans were building Fishbourne Palace? What about when tanks drove through the streets during World War Two? This book will uncover the important and exciting things that have happened in Sussex.

Some rather brainy folk have worked on this book to make sure it's fun and informative. So what are you waiting for? Peel back the pages and be amazed at Sussex's very own story.

Timeline shows which period (dates and people) each spread is talking about

Intriguing photos

THE FACTS

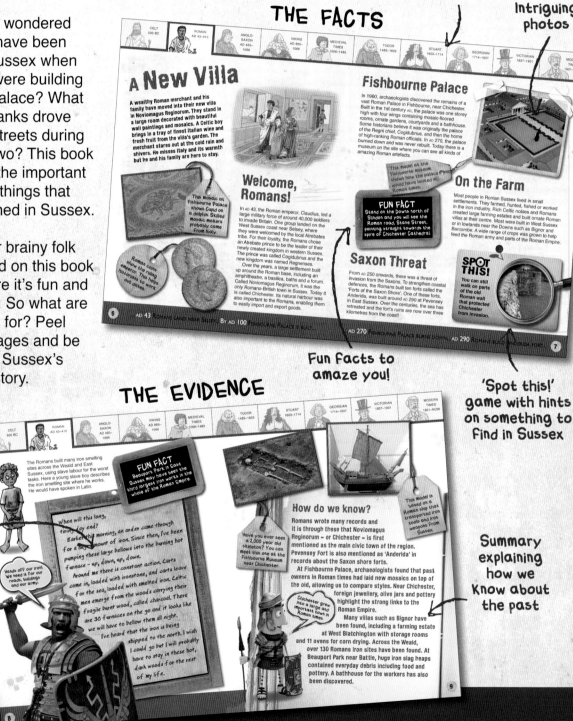

Fun facts to amaze you!

'Spot this!' game with hints on something to find in Sussex

THE EVIDENCE

Imaginary account of what it was like for children growing up in Sussex

Summary explaining how we know about the past

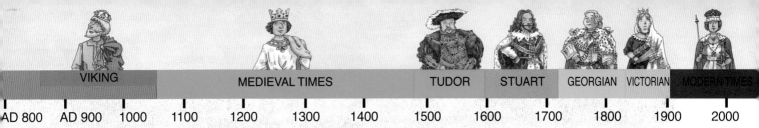

Contents

Back at the Roundhouse   4

A New Villa   6

Invaders!   10

Building a Castle   12

Battle Abbey   14

Smugglers!   16

The Railway Boom   22

Coming Home   26

Today and Tomorrow   28

Glossary   30
Index   31
Acknowledgements   32

Back at the Roundhouse

A young Celtic girl washes vegetables before adding them to a bubbling pot of stew. A light wind sweeps across the Downs, wafting smoke from the fire into the girl's eyes. It has been a long day. She has looked after her baby brother and the family's animals since early morning. Soon her parents will return from working in the fields, safe for the night inside their small settlement.

Roundhouse walls were made from woven branches covered in mud mixed with animal poo!

Raiders! Run for the hill fort! You can't miss it – it's dazzling white, thanks to the chalk banks.

Early Settlers

From 500 BC, Celtic tribes arrived to live in small settlements scattered across the Downs, along the coastal plains and in parts of the Weald Forest. Their huts were enclosed by earth-works, wooden fences or thick hedges. Celtic Downland farmers grew crops such as wheat and barley. They reared cattle, goats, sheep and pigs. Those near the coast fished using dugout wooden canoes. Settlers in the Weald Forest set up small iron-smelting works to make iron tools and weapons.

500 BC CELTIC TRIBES BUILD SMALL SETTLEMENTS ACROSS SOUTH DOWNS...

Hill Forts

The Celts built hill forts along the top of the South Downs. Early hill forts such as those at Wolstonbury and Caburn were quite small. Later hill forts, such as the Trundle, Cissbury Ring and Torberry, were much bigger and stronger. The forts were surrounded by deep ditches, massive banks of earth and tall wooden stakes for protection.

This Iron Age bracelet was discovered with the help of a metal detector in 2010 in Chichester.

FUN FACT
Cissbury Ring, near Worthing, is one of the biggest Celtic hill forts in Europe. Inside, it is over 26 hectares (the size of about 36 football pitches).

Celts were known for making pottery, colourful jewellery and fabrics.

Celtic Tribes

Towards the end of the Celtic period, small Sussex family tribes merged into three larger, more powerful tribes: the Atrebates, Cantiaci and the Belgae. As they were near to the sea, the tribes soon became wealthy, selling grain, salt, fish, pottery, wool, animal skins and iron to mainland Europe. Tribal chiefs were offered services and gifts in exchange for protection from other enemy tribes.

How do we know?

Along the South Downs, you can still see evidence of Celtic life from the remains of their hill forts. Recently, archaeologists found storage pits and post holes for round huts at Caburn and the Trundle, showing that they were also used as settlements. Iron farming tools, dug-out wooden canoes, weaving equipment and animal remains have also been excavated in settlements between the River Adur and River Ouse. Meanwhile 161 burial jars were found at Westhampnett in West Sussex, containing cremated remains of local Celtic people.

5

CELT 500 BC	ROMAN AD 43–410	ANGLO-SAXON AD 450–1066	VIKING AD 865–1066	MEDIEVAL TIMES 1066–1485

A New Villa

A wealthy Roman merchant and his family have moved into their new villa in Noviomagus Reginorum. They stand in a large room decorated with beautiful wall paintings and mosaics. A Celtic boy brings in a tray of finest Italian wine and fresh fruit from the villa's garden. The merchant stares out at the cold rain and shivers. He misses Italy and its warmth but he and his family are here to stay.

This mosaic at Fishbourne Palace shows Cupid on a dolphin. Skilled mosaic makers probably came from Italy.

Roman coins show the ruling emperor. This helps historians to work out dates.

Welcome, Romans!

In AD 43, the Roman emperor, Claudius, led a large military force of around 40,000 soldiers to invade Britain. One group landed on the West Sussex coast near Selsey, where they were welcomed by the local Atrebates tribe. For their loyalty, the Romans chose an Atrebate prince to be the leader of their newly created kingdom in western Sussex. The prince was called Cogidubnus and the new kingdom was named Regnenses.

Over the years, a large settlement built up around the Roman base, including an amphitheatre, a basilica, baths and a forum. Called Noviomagus Reginorum, it was the only Romano-British town in Sussex. Today it is called Chichester. Its natural harbour was also important to the Romans, enabling them to easily import and export goods.

Fishbourne Palace

In 1960, archaeologists discovered the remains of a vast Roman Palace in Fishbourne, near Chichester. Built in the 1st century AD, the palace was one storey high with four wings containing mosaic-floored rooms, ornate gardens, courtyards and a bathhouse. Some historians believe it was originally the palace of the Regni chief, Cogidubnus, and then the home of high-ranking Roman officials. In AD 270, the palace burned down and was never rebuilt. Today there is a museum on the site where you can see all kinds of amazing Roman artefacts.

This model at the Fishbourne museum shows how the palace would have looked in Roman times.

FUN FACT
Stand on the Downs north of Slindon and you will see the Roman road, Stane Street, pointing straight towards the spire of Chichester Cathedral.

On the Farm

Most people in Roman Sussex lived in small settlements. They farmed, hunted, fished or worked in the iron industry. Rich Celtic nobles and Romans created large farming estates and built ornate Roman villas at their centre. Most were built in West Sussex or in lowlands near the Downs such as Bignor and Barcombe. A wide range of crops was grown to help feed the Roman army and parts of the Roman Empire.

Saxon Threat

From AD 250 onwards, there was a threat of invasion from the Saxons. To strengthen coastal defences, the Romans built ten forts called the 'Forts of the Saxon Shore'. One of these forts, Anderida, was built around AD 290 at Pevensey in East Sussex. Over the centuries, the sea has retreated and the fort's ruins are now over three kilometres from the coast!

SPOT THIS!
You can still walk on parts of the old Roman wall that protected Chichester from invasion.

The Romans built many iron smelting sites across the Weald and East Sussex, using slave labour for the worst tasks. Here a young slave boy describes the iron smelting site where he works. He would have spoken in Latin.

FUN FACT
Beauport Park in East Sussex may have been the third largest iron works in the whole of the Roman Empire.

Hands off our iron! We need it for our roads, buildings and our army.

When will this long, tiring day end?

Earlier this morning, an order came through for a huge amount of iron. Since then, I've been pumping these large bellows into the burning hot furnace – up, down, up, down.

Around me there is constant action. Carts come in, loaded with ironstone, and carts leave for the sea, loaded with smelted iron. Celtic men emerge from the woods carrying their fragile burnt wood, called charcoal. There are 30 furnaces on the go and it looks like we will have to bellow them all night.

I've heard that the iron is being shipped to the north. I wish I could go but I will probably have to stay in these hot, dark woods for the rest of my life.

This model is based on a Roman ship that transported iron tools and iron weapons from Sussex.

Have you ever seen a 2,000 year old skeleton? You can meet this one at the Fishbourne Museum near Chichester.

How do we know?

Romans wrote many records and it is through these that Noviomagus Reginorum – or Chichester – is first mentioned as the main civic town of the region. Pevensey Fort is also mentioned as 'Anderida' in records about the Saxon shore forts.

At Fishbourne Palace, archaeologists found that past owners in Roman times had laid new mosaics on top of the old, allowing us to compare styles. Near Chichester, foreign jewellery, olive jars and pottery highlight the strong links to the Roman Empire.

Chichester grew into a large and important town in Roman times.

Many villas such as Bignor have been found, including a farming estate at West Blatchington with storage rooms and 11 ovens for corn drying. Across the Weald, over 130 Romans iron sites have been found. At Beauport Park near Battle, huge iron slag heaps contained everyday debris including food and pottery. A bathhouse for the workers has also been discovered.

9

Invaders!

The Saxons are here! Run for your lives! A Romano-British family who have lived here peacefully for many years flee their home for the safety of the big forest in the north. Leaving everything behind, a young woman grabs a stick and steers her geese through the mud. Everyone is beginning to panic – life will never be the same again.

SAXON PLACE NAMES

-borough	fortified place or hill
-borne	stream
-combe	valley
-ey	island or marsh land
-ham	village or homestead
-hurst	small wood
-tun, -ton or -stone	an enclosure or village
-worth	small farm

↑ How many of these can you find around Sussex?

Many Sussex places have Anglo-Saxon origins. Look out for place names containing the above.

A Saxon Kingdom

In the 5th century, most of the Roman army had left Britain, making it easy for the Saxons to attack the coastline. From AD 477, the Saxons invaded and settled in most of Sussex, apart from the area around Hastings which was occupied by another group of invaders called the Haestingas.

Killing or driving the Romano-British out of their homes into the Weald Forest, the Anglo-Saxons built their new farming communities along the coast, valleys and plains. Old Roman villas, the Wealden iron-works and Roman roads were left to crumble as Sussex became the 'Kingdom of the South Saxons'.

Place Names

In Sussex most place names ending with 'ing' start with the names of their Saxon settlers. For example, Worthing's original name, Wurthingas, meant 'Wurth's people' and Fletching is thought to be named after the people of Flecci. Other places were named after local features, such as Lewes, which means hills.

Pagan Beliefs

The South Saxons were the last Anglo-Saxon group to hold onto their pagan beliefs. In AD 681, their newly Christian king, King Ethelwalch, invited a bishop called Wilfrid to convert his people to Christianity and offered him land near Selsey for a monastery. At this time, there was a big famine in Sussex so Wilfrid's teachings and ideas for better fishing and farming methods made him popular with the South Saxons. Within five years, the kingdom had become Christian and wooden churches had been built within the settlements. After his death in about AD 710, Bishop Wilfrid was named a saint.

SPOT THIS!

St Andrew's Church in Bishopstone was built around AD 800. It may be the oldest Saxon church in Sussex.

Viking Threat

In the 9th century, a great danger appeared – the Vikings. To protect Sussex, King Alfred the Great built fortified towns called Burhs in Chichester, Burpham, Lewes, Pevensey and Hastings. He asked the local people to defend them. For a while life was peaceful but from AD 994 the Vikings returned. They ravaged the Sussex countryside until King Canute came to the throne in 1016.

The Anglo-Saxon Chronicle is a record of events in Saxon England. It was handwritten by monks.

How do we know?

The Anglo-Saxon Chronicle tells us about the South Saxons, including their invasion of Sussex, their chiefs and their battles. It also tells us about the Haestingas tribe in the east and about St Wilfrid's visit to Selsey. Excavated graves reveal a lot about Saxon Sussex. The Saxons believed they could take their belongings with them after death and were therefore buried with their most precious possessions. Artefacts discovered inside Sussex's Saxon graves include jewellery, shield bosses and vases.

11

Building a Castle

A young Saxon boy glares angrily at his new master who is shouting out orders. Since the Battle of Hastings, the boy and the men in his village have had to work non-stop, building a wooden castle on top of a huge mound of earth. A wooden fence encloses the large area where the castle's servants and soldiers will live. The boy sighs, and gets on with his work.

Battle of Hastings

In 1066, William, Duke of Normandy, decided to invade England. Landing at Pevensey, the large Norman army raided and burned houses around Hastings. The new king, Harold, had put together an army of men, many of them from Sussex, and marched to meet the Normans. The men fought in the hills behind Hastings, close to today's town of Battle. The Normans won, Harold was killed, and William became king of England.

Five Barons

After the Norman Conquest, William the Conqueror split Sussex into five regions called Rapes and gave each one to a loyal Norman baron. Within each Rape, the barons built motte and bailey castles that overlooked a river or port and small defence posts against attacks. The Saxons had to pay rent for land that was once theirs.

You can still see Arundel's motte and bailey castle today. Go and see it, I tell you!

Off to Market

In 1247, East Grinstead was granted a market charter allowing it to hold weekly markets and a yearly fair. Market charters attracted traders to a town where they could sell their goods without paying taxes and buyers who could get cheaper prices. Towns such as Heathfield and Horsham soon became wealthy, offering goods such as fish, textiles, livestock, corn and French wine.

SPOT THIS!
The Battle of Lewes' monument in Priory Park, Lewes, shows scenes of a 1264 battle.

FUN FACT
Battle Abbey was built in 1070 to remember those who died at the Battle of Hastings. It was built on the site of the battle.

Wealthy Ports

From the 11th century onwards, the port of Hastings was important for trade, warfare and transport to mainland Europe. It was allowed to charge tolls and not pay taxes, in exchange for supplying ships and crew. Ports at Rye and Winchelsea were also important and, with the need for warships due to the French wars, the Sussex ports became wealthy. But by Tudor times, the harbours had silted up and the navy had moved to Portsmouth. The ports were in decline.

Sussex was made up of lots of small villages at this time.

How do we know?

Castles, churches, monastery ruins, houses and ports from medieval Sussex still survive today. At Arundel and Lewes you can see the mounds of motte and bailey castles. Weald and Downland Open Air Museum has fine examples of medieval houses built in Sussex. The Domesday Book and images from the Bayeux Tapestry also help to give us an idea of what medieval Sussex was like.

Battle Abbey

A monk falls to his knees as Henry VIII's soldiers smash Battle Abbey's priceless glass windows. The king is taking the land and treasures of many Sussex monasteries and abbeys. As he prays, the young monk smells the ornate wooden roofs burn above him. For over 400 years the abbey has played an important part in the lives of the monks and local people. Soon the abbey will be gone and the monk will be homeless.

A Raided Place

In 1534, Henry VIII created the Church of England in order to divorce his first wife. He began closing down, or 'dissolving', the monasteries. Battle Abbey, Lewes Priory and other Sussex monasteries were raided and destroyed, and many people lost their lives.

Life in Tudor times was also unsettled on the Sussex coast, which was regularly attacked by the French at this time. One of the worst raids was on the fishing town of Brighthelmstone (Brighton) in 1514. French raiders came ashore and ransacked the town, burning down its wooden houses.

The people of Brighton rebuilt their town and set up beacons as a warning system for future raids. This proved to be a success when, in 1545, the town's people and nearby villagers came together and drove French raiders away.

After the French raid on Brighton, the only building left standing was the stone church of St Nicholas.

The Martyrs

During the reign of Mary I, a total of 287 men and women were burned at the stake for not following the Catholic faith. From 1555 to 1557, burnings took place in East Grinstead, Mayfield, Lewes and Steyning. The memory of the 17 'Sussex Martyrs' burned in Lewes is still celebrated with annual torchlight processions, attracting thousands of people. Bonfire societies carry 17 barrels of burning tar and 17 flaming crosses every year on 5th November.

When Elizabeth I became queen, she wanted everyone to be Protestant. She ordered Catholics to be persecuted. In 1588, two men were executed in Chichester for not following the Protestant faith. This was a difficult time for people living in Sussex.

Most iron cannons were made in Sussex. The first one came from Buxted in 1543.

Wealden Iron

In the 1540s, a new iron-smelting method at higher temperatures created better iron. This meant using more charcoal for fuel. With a forest full of wood and iron ore, the Weald became the major iron producer in England. From 1543, over 180 iron works produced thousands of cannons, weapons and everyday iron products. The iron and wood were also used for house building, ship building and the glass industry. So many trees were cut down that a large part of the Weald Forest disappeared.

SPOT THIS!

The home of author Rudyard Kipling, in Burwash, was built for an ironmaster in the 17th century.

How do we know?

Pamphlets and illustrations give us an insight into the beliefs, trials and terrible executions of the 'Sussex Martyrs', as well as events such as the French raids. Many large Tudor and Stuart houses were built during this time, such as Parham House and the fine ironmaster houses. The Anne of Cleves House in Sussex has a good display about the iron industry and shows artefacts such as fire backs and cannons. The ruins of Battle Abbey and Lewes Priory can also still be seen today.

Smugglers!

Winds howl as huge, towering waves crash onto a bay near Beachy Head. This does not stop the six men from their work. A ship has just smashed against the cliffs, spilling its cargo of tea and other goods into the sea. A young man staggers up the steep beach with a heavy barrel on his shoulder. He and his gang must get the loot to the village as soon as possible. On the cliffs, two customs officers watch quietly. Is this the end for these smugglers?

Smuggling Gangs

Smuggling in Sussex reached its peak in the 18th century. High taxes were put on goods coming into England so smuggling them past customs officers to sell at cheaper prices became a big industry. Many of the smuggling gangs were unemployed or part-time workers but quite often whole villages were involved, including the vicar and the local lord. Where there were tall cliffs, goods were winched up or slung across a smuggler's back who would then be pulled up on a rope.

By the 1820s, tougher laws had stopped most smuggling but smugglers such as the Mayfield Gang and the Hawkhurst Gang are still remembered in Sussex today.

(COOL!)

The Seven Stars Inn at Robertsbridge was often visited by the notorious Hawkhurst Gang.

SPOT THIS!

The Smugglers' Stone in Broyle Road, Chichester, marks the grave of a convicted smuggler.

Better Roads

Until the mid-18th century, the roads in Sussex were in a terrible state. In 1749, the Sussex Turnpike Trust was set up to repair the road from Hindhead to Chichester. Soon other turnpike trusts were set up along the main roads of East and West Sussex. Toll gates were built across the road every three kilometres. With better roads, a bustling stagecoach industry developed as rich visitors flocked to the sea.

Farming Estates

During the 18th century, the population was growing fast and more food was needed to feed the people. In Sussex, big estates were created to farm the Downs and coastal plains. Farmers and wealthy landowners used a large workforce of poor and seasonal workers from the local areas. The third Lord Egremont designed a successful farm on his Petworth estate, where he used the new method of rotating crops such as turnips, wheat, barley, oats, grass and potatoes. He also introduced new machinery to make some jobs quicker and cheaper.

Eastbourne's Martello Tower was built in 1800–1802 to defend the coast from a French invasion. Today it's a museum.

FUN FACT
More windmills were built in the 1820s to cope with the increased demand for corn. There were 16 in Hastings and 12 on the Downs near Brighton.

A Miracle Cure

By the mid-18th century, Brighton had turned from a wealthy fishing port into a poor settlement ravaged by the terrible storms of 1703 and 1705. However, in 1750, it was made popular by Dr Richard Russell from Lewes, who wrote about a wonderful cure for ill health – bathing and drinking sea water. In 1753, he set up a clinic in Brighton and, as it was not too far from London, the rich flocked down to take the fresh air, bathe and drink the special sea medicine. It was a big turning point in the fortunes of Brighton and many towns and villages along the Sussex coast.

Dr Russell's Famous Sea Water Cure

Woodlice
Cuttlefish bones
Crab's eyes
Bicarbonate of soda
Milk
Sea water

SPOT THIS!

Can you spot this plaque on the Royal Albion Hotel in Brighton? It marks where Dr Russell had his clinic.

ON THIS SITE STOOD RUSSELL HOUSE WHERE LIVED FROM 1759 RICHARD RUSSELL M.D.,F.R.S. IF YOU SEEK HIS MONUMENT LOOK AROUND

Fishing to Tourism

Many of Brighton's fishing families often found extra work on the local farms or as smugglers but as Dr Russell's spa became popular, they began to look after the rich visitors. Some set up guest houses, ballrooms, coaching inns, shops and eating houses while others worked as cleaners, cooks, gardeners or grooms.

Ladies and gentlemen would go to separate beaches where the gentlemen would be helped into the sea by men called 'bathers' and the ladies helped in by women called 'dippers'. Martha Gunn was known as the queen of the dippers and became famous in Georgian Brighton.

People changed into their bathing clothes inside bathing machines, which were then wheeled into the sea.

Regency Brighton

From 1783, the son of King George III, also called George, became a regular visitor to Brighton. He stayed in a house called the Marine Pavilion and loved partying. With this royal connection, Brighton became the height of fashion and grew very fast. Theatres, shops, banks, coffee houses, hotels, Brighton Racecourse, a hospital and beautiful houses such as those in Kemp Town were some of the many improvements.

In 1821, Sake Dean Mohamed opened the first 'shampooing vapour baths' in Brighton.

The Pavilion changed a lot in design and size between 1787 and 1823.

FUN FACT
Before the 1780s the Old Steine was used for drying fishing nets. It was then turned into walks and gardens for the Royal Pavilion.

Not another stagecoach! I've already got my hands full!

Stagecoaches

With more and more visitors coming to Brighton from London, Sussex benefited in an unexpected way – from stagecoaches. As the roads improved, stagecoach journeys to the coast became quicker and more popular. Towns such as East Grinstead, Crawley, Horsham and Lewes thrived as main coaching stops, and so did the small inns in villages along the route. Places like Hastings, Worthing, Littlehampton and Eastbourne also welcomed many rich visitors and increased in wealth.

The son of King George III became Prince Regent to help rule the country while his father was ill. In 1815, the Prince Regent ordered Brighton Pavilion to be redesigned and enlarged so he could use it for parties and music evenings. Here, a young lady writes to her sister about a dinner party held there.

The Pavilion is very odd indeed. There are Chinese dragons everywhere!

Dearest Grace,

It is 3am in the morning and Mama and I have just returned from an amazing dinner party hosted by the Prince Regent at his Brighton Pavilion. On the outside, the Pavilion looks like an Indian Palace but on the inside, everything is Chinese.

When all the guests had arrived, the Prince Regent led us into the Banqueting Hall. What a room! Over the dining table there hung a dazzling chandelier, held up by a huge Chinese dragon.

When we were all seated, the footmen brought us 30 different dishes of food. Never before have I eaten so much! Mama claims that when the Grand Duke of Russia visited in 1817, they had over 100 different dishes. No wonder the Prince Regent is so fat!

After dinner we talked, played cards and listened to music until our carriages arrived. I hope one day you can come with me to the Pavilion and we can count all the dragons together.

Your loving sister,

Frances

FUN FACT
The Dome Theatre near the Pavilion was originally the Prince Regent's stables, with space for 44 horses!

How do we know?

What we know about the smugglers of Sussex mainly comes from old local stories, pictures, court proceedings and letters. Hastings Museum has one of the biggest collections about smuggling in Sussex with displays of artefacts.

Look out along the main roads for old toll houses and stagecoach inns such as the White Hart Inn in Crawley. Some inns still have their wide entrances which carriages used to go through.

The original paintings, plans and drawings of the Royal Pavilion designers have helped historians restore the rooms to their former glory. Colours, wallpaper, lights, furniture, mirrors and decorations have all been faithfully copied. You can see a lot of these pictures at Brighton Museum or in the Pavilion.

The Prince Regent held extravagant parties at Brighton Pavilion. He became King George IV in 1820.

Brighton's rich and royal visitors made the town a fashionable and wealthy place in Georgian times.

Kemp Town was built by Thomas Reed Kemp. It was finished in 1853, taking 30 years to complete.

21

The Railway Boom

Everyone cheers and waves as the gleaming red locomotive moves slowly into the new railway station. The air is filled with steam and the smell of burning coal. Beneath the noise of the engine is the sound of the town's church bells, ringing out in celebration. The excited crowd moves forward, eager to see the amazing horseless carriage and its passengers. Hastings is welcoming its first visitors from London.

New Railways

Eleven million bricks were used to build the Balcombe Viaduct over the River Ouse.

In 1841, the London to Brighton railway line was opened. It took over 6,000 men, 962 horses and 13 engines to build the line, which included railway stations, five tunnels and the Balcombe Viaduct. Soon railway lines were being laid all over Sussex, linking towns and villages to London and the rest of the south east.

Many of the railway builders were local Sussex men who had been unemployed or had left their farming, fishing or craft jobs to earn more money. They lived in huts or were put up in cottages near to the line.

Come and Visit!

The new railway lines brought more visitors to Sussex. New and old market towns grew as they attracted more businesses and visitors to their market days. Seaside resorts such as Hastings and Worthing became popular with daytrippers, and sea trade boomed at the ports of Newhaven and Shoreham.

The railways also brought new opportunities. Railway companies needed signalmen, drivers, guards, carriage builders and station staff. Or you could work in the building industry or in shops, hotels and restaurants at the seaside.

SPOT THIS!

This clock tower in Brighton was built in Victorian times. Can you spot it on North Street?

FUN FACT

In 1874, 70 kilometres of sewers were laid under Brighton. Today you can go on a tour of the sewers to see the skills of the builders.

30,000 sheep in one place at the same time? Ewe must be joking.

Poor Sussex

Living conditions for the families of poor agricultural labourers could be very bad. They often lived in damp, dark cottages without running water, sewers or power apart from candles or small amounts of coal. Workhouses were set up to take the destitute but these too were often harsh. Many people left to find work in the big towns, which soon became overcrowded and unhealthy. However, from the 1870s, things began to improve with proper sewers, clean water, hospitals and better housing.

Fields and Sheep

In Victorian times, most people still worked in farming. Some had small farms called smallholdings but most were employed by landowners on big estates. With a growing population, most of the land in Sussex was given over to growing crops. The South Downs were also covered by the famous Sussex Downland Sheep, known for their wool and meat. On annual fair days, the sheep farmers would guide them through the lanes to be sold. In Lewes, up to 30,000 sheep would be brought to the fair.

Railway journeys were quick and cheap, meaning that for the first time working-class people could come to Sussex, enjoy trips to the seaside and visit the pleasure gardens. Here a young boy called Alf writes in his diary, describing a day trip to the seaside.

I had never seen the sea before. Now I've paddled in it!

> **23rd August, 1899**
>
> Today Mum, Dad, Elsie and I went to the seaside on the train. When we arrived, we followed the crowd to the beach. Elsie and I had a great time splashing and paddling in the cold sea and building sandcastles. Mine was the best!
>
> Dad took us up to the pier to get Penny Licks. The Italian man scooped vanilla ice cream into glass jars which we licked clean and gave back to him. Yum! On the way back, we stopped to watch a Punch and Judy show.
>
> Before we left for home, Mum and Dad went to see a show at the end of pier, while we collected coloured pebbles as souvenirs.
>
> I will always remember the smell of smoke from the magic lantern and the sound of the seagulls and bands. I hope we go to the seaside again soon.

Brighton West Pier was built in 1866. Today only its skeleton is left, after a fire in 2003.

Volks Railway was the world's first electric railway.

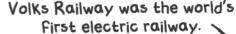

VOLKS ELECTRIC RAILWAY
THE OLDEST ELECTRIC RAILWAY IN THE WORLD STILL OPERATING - OPENED 4TH AUGUST 1883
FREQUENT TRAINS TO AND FROM THE MARINA STATION

TUDOR 1485–1603	STUART 1603–1714	GEORGIAN 1714–1837	VICTORIAN 1837–1901	MODERN TIMES 1901–NOW

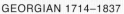

People wore very different clothes to the seaside in Victorian times! This is a Sussex beach in 1895.

This is a Victorian camera. The leather bellows were moved in or out to change the focus.

How do we know?

From 1841, a law was passed to take a census of details about every household in the country on a certain day every ten years. By comparing censuses, we can see who had changed occupations, who had left the area and who stayed.

Railway reports, books, newspaper reports, rail plans and records also tell us a lot about the railways. Early rail company records show that many employees were born in Sussex but only 30% of engine drivers came from there due to a lack of skills.

Photographs, old newspapers, posters, postcards, adverts, souvenirs and the remaining Victorian parks or buildings give us a sense of how Victorian children spent their leisure time.

Visitors flocked to Sussex during Victorian times, thanks to the new railways.

Coming Home

A large boat has docked at a Sussex port, packed with injured soldiers returning from action at the front line in France. They quietly wait their turn to disembark while a soldier on a stretcher is quickly carried off to an awaiting ambulance. A young gunner holds his heavily bandaged head as he is helped down the gangplank by a nurse. He is glad to be back and wonders when he will see his family again in their quiet Sussex village.

The Chattri on the Downs is a memorial to Indian soldiers who died during World War One.

World War One

During World War One, Sussex was one of the first counties to receive badly injured soldiers from the front lines. Once the hospitals were full, large buildings such as hotels, asylums and grand houses were turned into wards. Brighton Pavilion was turned into a military hospital to care for over 4,000 Indian soldiers and over 6,000 other soldiers. Sussex villages lost many young men in the war.

A Second War

Sussex was badly affected by air raids in World War Two because of its position and the large number of Allied forces based there. Eastbourne experienced the worst bombing, with 174 people killed. In 1943, a bomb fell on the Whitehall Cinema in East Grinstead, killing 108 people.

As women and children were evacuated out of the seaside towns, Allied troops came in. The RAF Tangmere Base near Chichester was an important base for the fighter pilots who fought in the Battle of Britain in 1940.

...1943 BOMB HITS EAST GRINSTEAD CINEMA...1944 D-DAY TROOPS HIDE OUT IN SUSSEX...

Beach Defences

Sussex's close location to mainland Europe made it a perfect place for a German invasion. As a result the coast was heavily defended, with old castles such as Pevensey strengthened, and some of the Martello Towers used as observation and gun posts. Beaches were mined and blocked off with barbed wire. Newhaven Fort became a major military base with secret tunnels holding a major communication station.

As D-Day approached on 6th June, 1944, thousands of Allied and British soldiers were secretly billeted in areas such as Cuckfield, Ditchling, Bexhill, Seaford, Chichester and Shoreham. Tanks and vehicles were hidden under trees and bushes, and locals were told not to talk to anyone about the preparations. On the day of the invasion, many of the 7,000 boats that took soldiers to France were from Sussex.

SPOT THIS!

Pillboxes were built across Sussex during World War Two. Can you spot this one at Cuckmere Haven?

After the War

In 1974, Sussex was officially divided into two counties: East Sussex and West Sussex. West Sussex with its more developed transport network has a bigger population and larger economy but both counties have their own distinct wealth of traditions, history, natural beauty and friendly people.

The Queen Victoria Hospital in East Grinstead treated badly burned World War Two pilots.

How do we know?

Evidence of wartime Sussex includes old photographs, written army records, news reels, newspapers, films, letters and artefacts such as rationing books and gas masks. First-hand accounts from people who lived through the wars are very useful. Does anyone in your family remember World War Two? Brighton has recently produced an oral history of World War Two where people have recorded their wartime experiences, such as the occasion when a girl escaped the bombing of her local cinema.

Today and Tomorrow

We can find out a lot about the history of Sussex from resources such as objects from archaeological digs, buildings, written records, pictures, songs, maps, oral accounts and photographs. But what will we pass on to people in the future?

⬆ The London to Brighton Vintage Car Race has been run every November since 1896, apart from during wartime. People enjoy seeing the old cars from the past.

◀ The current Brighton Pier used to be called the Palace Pier. Will another pier replace it one day?

You should feel proud to be from Sussex. You're making history!

◀ Shoreham Port is a thriving port which caters for large cargo ships and different marine activities. Will it still be a port in the future or could it be affected by rising sea levels?

TUDOR 1485–1603	STUART 1603–1714	GEORGIAN 1714–1837	VICTORIAN 1837–1901	MODERN TIMES 1901–NOW

⬆ Gatwick Airport was a racecourse 100 years ago. What could it be in another 100 years' time?

⬆ The South Downs National Park has been formed to protect the land and wildlife from future development or harm.

⬅ Brighton and Hove Albion Football Club's new stadium has been designed to fit in with the countryside. Do you think the design is successful?

⬆ Millions of people visit the Sussex coast every year. Some are attracted to big seaside towns such as Eastbourne, while others prefer quieter areas such as the Witterings or Rye.

How will they know?

Today there are many ways in which information is recorded for the future. Modern technology ensures that millions of first-hand accounts, photographs, pieces of art and music and thoughts of everyday life will be preserved to give future generations a strong understanding of what Sussex is like for us, now.

Glossary

Abbey – a building where monks or nuns live and work.

AD – a short way to write anno Domini, which is Latin and means 'in the year of Our Lord', i.e. after the birth of Christ.

Allied – united or friendly (on the same side as us in a war).

Amphitheatre – a round open-air theatre, surrounded by seats that rise from the centre so everyone can see and hear.

Archaeologist – someone who studies the past by examining buildings and objects left behind by previous people and cultures.

Artefact – an object, often an archaeological one.

Basilica – a Roman building used for public offices.

BC – these initials mean Before Christ and are used for the time before Jesus Christ was born.

Bellows – two handles that are pumped to blow air onto a fire to make the flames bigger.

Boss – a round ornamental stud, often found on the end of a shield or on a ceiling.

Catholic – or Roman Catholic: a member of the Christian religion that has the Pope at its head.

Charter – written permission to do something.

Christian – a person who believes that Jesus Christ is the son of God and follows his teachings.

Church of England – a Christian religion headed by the king or queen.

Destitute – poor to the point of having absolutely nothing.

Domesday Book – a record of who owned property, land, people and animals in 11th century Britain.

Evacuate – having to leave your home and live somewhere else for safety.

Excavate – to dig up buried objects in order to find out about the past.

Famine – a shortage of food so bad that people starve to death.

Forum – a meeting or place where people discuss things.

Furnace – like a very big oven, used for burning rubbish or melting metals.

Latin – the language of ancient Rome and the foundation of many other languages.

Monastery – a place where monks live and worship.

Mosaic – small pieces of coloured glass or stone stuck together to form a design.

Oral – anything spoken.

Pagan – someone who believes in more than one god.

Persecute – to abuse someone, because of their race or religion.

Pillbox – a small military hide-out, usually made of concrete.

Port – a place, next to land, where the water is deep enough for ships to stop and stay.

Protestant – a member of the Christian religion that considers the king or queen of England to be the head of its church.

Ration book – a book containing tokens used to buy rations of food during World War Two.

Sewer – underground pipes where all human waste goes.

Silt – fine mud.

Smuggler – someone bringing goods into a country in secret to avoid paying tax on them.

Toll – a charge or tax for using a road, river or bridge.

Index

Alfred the Great, 11
Anderida (Pevensey) fort, 7, 9
Anglo-Saxon Chronicle, the, 11
Anne of Cleves House, the, 15
Arundel Castle, 12
Atrebates tribe, 5, 6

Balcombe Viaduct, 22
Barcombe Downs, 7
Battle, 12
Battle Abbey, 12, 13, 14, 15
Battle of Britain, 26
Battle of Hastings, 12, 13
Bayeux Tapestry, 13
Beachy Head, 16
Beauport Park, 8, 9
Belgae tribe, 5
Bignor Downs, 7
Bignor Palace, 9
Brighton and Hove Albion
    Football Club, 29
Brighton Racecourse, 19
Brighton Royal Pavilion, 19, 20,
    21, 26
Brighton West Pier, 24

Caburn hill fort, 5
Cantiaci tribe, 5
Chattri, the, 26
Chichester Cathedral, 7
Cissbury Ring hill fort, 5
Claudius, 6
Cogidubnus, 6, 7
Cuckmere Haven Pillbox, 27

D-Day, 26, 27
Dissolution of the Monasteries,
    14
Domesday Book, the, 13

East Grinstead bombing, 26
Elizabeth I, 15

Ethelwalch, 11

Falmer Football Stadium, 28
Fishbourne Museum, 7, 9
Fishbourne Palace, 6, 7, 9
Fletching, 10
French raids, the, 15

Gatwick Airport, 29
George I, 16
George II, 17
George III, 19
George IV, 21
Gunn, Martha, 18

Harold, 12
Hastings Museum, 21
Hawkhurst Gang, the, 16
Henry VIII, 14

Kemp, Thomas Reed, 21
Kemp Town, 19, 21
Kipling, Rudyard, 15

Lewes Priory, 14, 15
London to Brighton Railway, 22,
    23
London to Brighton Vintage Car
    Race, 28

Marine Pavilion, 19
Martello Towers, 27
Martello Tower Museum, 17
Mary I, 15
Mayfield Gang, the, 16
Mohamed, Sake Dean, 19

Newhaven Fort, 27
Norman Conquest, 12

Old Roman wall, 7
Old Steine, the, 19

Palace Pier, 28
Parham House, 15
Pevensey Castle, 27
Pevensey (Anderida) fort, 7, 9
Prince Regent (George IV), 19,
    20

Queen Victoria Hospital, the, 27

RAF Tangmere Base, 26
River Adur, 5
River Ouse, 5, 22
Royal Albion Hotel, Brighton,
    the, 18
Russell, Dr Richard, 18

Saxon invasion, 7, 10
St Wilfrid, 11
St Nicholas Church, 14
Seven Stars Inn, the, 16
Shoreham Port, 28
Smugglers' Stone, the, 17
South Downs, 4, 5
South Downs National Park,
    the, 29
Sussex Martyrs, the, 15
Sussex Turnpike Trust, 17

Torberry hill fort, 5
Trundle hill fort, 5

Volks Electric Railway, 24

Weald and Downland Open Air
    Museum, 13
Weald Forest, 4, 10, 15
William I (William the
    Conqueror), 12
Wolstonbury hill fort, 5
World War One, 26
World War Two, 26, 27

Acknowledgements

The publishers would like to thank the following people and organizations
for their permission to reproduce material on the following pages:

p1: Adrian Pink/Flickr; p5: Portable Antiquities Scheme; p6: Fishbourne Roman Palace; p7: Fishbourne Roman Palace, Nick Drury/Flickr; p9: Fishbourne Roman Palace; p11: Gary Shield/Flickr; p13: Howard Stanbury/Flickr; p15: Linda Spashett/Wikipedia; p16: John Law/Flickr; p17: www.westsussex.info, Adrian Pink/Flickr; p18: Angelo Hornak/Alamy; p21: Wikipedia, Tom Bastin/Flickr; p22: Henry Law/Flickr; p25: Swindon Museum, Mary Evans Picture Library/Gerald Wilson; p26: Latitude Stock/Alamy; p27: UKgeofan/Wikipedia; p28: David Hone/Flickr, Barry Searle/Flickr; p29: Mark Wordingham/Flickr, Martin Roell/Flickr, Dominic Alves/Wikipedia, Mark Wills/Flickr.

All other images copyright of Hometown World

Every effort has been made to trace and acknowledge the ownership of copyright.
If any rights have been omitted, the publishers offer to rectify this in any future editions.

Written by Alison Milford
Edited by Gemma Cary
Educational consultant: Neil Thompson
Local history consultant: Mark Hoult
Designed by Sarah Allen

Illustrated by Kate Davies, Dynamo Ltd, Virginia Gray,
Leighton Noyes, Nick Shewring and Tim Sutcliffe.
Additional photographs by Alex Long

First published by HOMETOWN WORLD in 2012
Hometown World Ltd
7 Northumberland Buildings
Bath BA1 2JB

www.hometownworld.co.uk

CELT	ROMAN	ANGLO-SAXON	VIKING	MEDIEVAL TIMES
500 BC	AD 43–410	AD 450–1066	AD 865–1066	1066–1485